BLACK GIRL'S
MANUAL

to
FINANCIAL BREAKTHROUGH

Guide to build wealth, Retire in advance and Make your dream life a reality

Bianca Robert

Table of Contents

Introduction

In a world where financial independence is a gateway to limitless opportunities and a life filled with dreams realized, there exists a unique journey that Black women embark upon—a journey marked by resilience, innovation, and strength. The "Black Girl's Manual to Financial Breakthrough" is not just a guide; it is a celebration of the power and potential that resides within each and every Black woman seeking to redefine her financial future. This book is dedicated to empowering Black girls, women, and anyone who wishes to join us on this transformative journey towards financial prosperity.

The path to financial empowerment often takes a winding course, influenced by a multitude of external factors and personal experiences. For Black girls and women, this journey can be compounded by historical disparities, systemic barriers, and cultural dynamics. Yet, within this landscape, there is an immense wellspring of ambition, resilience, and unyielding determination that is driving a generation of Black women to shatter the glass ceiling and secure their financial destinies. This book is a testament to that spirit—a guiding light to illuminate the way towards financial success.

Understanding the nuances of finance and wealth building is essential, but equally important is recognizing the uniqueness of each individual's journey. Whether you're starting from scratch, striving to escape the shackles of debt, or looking to accelerate your path to retirement, this manual is tailored to meet you where you are. It is designed to empower you with the knowledge and strategies needed to transcend your financial limitations and unlock a world of possibilities.

In these pages, we will delve into the foundations of financial literacy, setting meaningful goals, and creating a robust financial framework. We will explore the art of smart budgeting, effective saving, and the transformative potential of investment. We will embrace the pursuit of multiple streams of income, the entrepreneurial spirit that fuels innovation, and the power of financial independence.

Moreover, we'll confront the challenges unique to Black women when it comes to finances. We'll explore ways to navigate debt, build strong credit, protect your financial future, and design a retirement plan that allows you to retire on your terms.

As we journey together, we'll not only tackle financial concepts and strategies but also address the deep seated beliefs, mindsets, and attitudes that can either empower or hinder your progress. We'll help you break through limiting beliefs, face financial setbacks with resilience, and build a supportive network that understands your journey.

This manual is more than just words on paper; it is a blueprint for transforming your financial reality. It's a declaration of your right to financial success and a proclamation of the strength and determination that defines you. It is the guiding star that will lead you towards a future where your dreams are not only within reach but firmly in your grasp.

The "Black Girl's Manual to Financial Breakthrough" is a testament to the remarkable journey of Black women who aspire to build wealth, retire in advance, and make their dream lives a reality. It is your guide, your ally, and your source of inspiration on the path to financial empowerment. So, let us embark on this transformative journey together, celebrating our uniqueness and embracing our shared destiny—a destiny where your financial breakthrough is not just a dream but a vivid and triumphant reality.

Chapter 1

Understanding Your Financial Landscape

To build a strong financial future and attain the wealth and security you desire, it's essential to begin by understanding your current financial landscape. This chapter is your starting point, where we explore the power of financial literacy and strategies for overcoming financial barriers that may stand in your way.

The Power of Financial Literacy

Financial literacy is not just a buzzword; it is the cornerstone of financial empowerment. In this section, we delve into the significance of financial literacy and how it can be a transformative force in your life.

- **Understanding the Impact of Financial Knowledge on Decision-Making**

Financial knowledge is a powerful tool that can significantly influence your decision-making process in various aspects of your life. Here's an indepth look at the impact of financial knowledge on decision-making:

1. Informed Decision-Making

- Financial knowledge equips you with a solid understanding of various financial concepts, from budgeting to investing.
- Informed decisions are based on facts and data, which reduce the chances of impulsive or ill informed choices.

2. Improved Financial Planning

- With financial knowledge, you can create comprehensive financial plans that align with your goals and aspirations.
- You'll be better prepared to set realistic financial targets and devise a roadmap to achieve them.

3. Risk Management

- Understanding financial risks and how to mitigate them is a key aspect of decision-making.
- Financial knowledge enables you to assess risks associated with investments, loans, or other financial transactions.

4. Confidence in Financial Choices

- Financial literacy instills confidence in your financial decisions.
- When you understand the implications of your choices, you're more likely to stand by your decisions even in the face of uncertainty.

5. LongTerm Financial Security

- Financial knowledge helps you make choices that contribute to long term financial security.
- You'll be more likely to save for retirement, build emergency funds, and protect your assets.

6. Avoiding Costly Mistakes

- Lack of financial knowledge can lead to costly mistakes, such as accumulating debt, falling for scams, or making poor investment decisions.
- With financial literacy, you can steer clear of these pitfalls.

7. Empowerment and Independence

- Financial knowledge empowers you to take control of your financial destiny.
- It reduces reliance on others for financial decisions and enables you to

make choices that align with your values and goals.

8. Enhanced Quality of Life

- Making sound financial decisions can lead to a higher quality of life.
- Financial knowledge allows you to prioritize what matters most to you, whether it's homeownership, education, travel, or philanthropy.

The impact of financial knowledge on decision-making cannot be overstated. It empowers you to make informed, confident choices that lead to improved financial well-being and a brighter future. By arming yourself with financial knowledge, you'll be better equipped to navigate the complex financial landscape and make decisions that align with your dreams and aspirations.

- **Building a Strong Financial Foundation**

A strong financial foundation is the bedrock upon which your financial success is built. In this section, we'll explore the key elements and strategies for constructing a solid financial base that supports your journey towards wealth and financial security.

1. Budgeting and Money Management
Creating a Budget
- The importance of setting up a budget to track your income and expenses.
- Tips for creating a realistic and effective budget that aligns with your financial goals.

Expense Tracking
- Strategies for monitoring your spending habits.
- Identifying areas where you can cut costs and redirect funds toward your financial objectives.

Emergency Funds
- The role of an emergency fund in financial stability.
- How to establish and maintain an emergency fund for unexpected expenses.

2. Saving Strategies for Success
Setting Savings Goal
- The significance of setting clear and achievable savings goals.
- Differentiating between shortterm and longterm savings objectives.

Automated Savings
- The advantages of automating your savings.
- How to set up automatic transfers to savings accounts or investment portfolios.

Debt Management
- Understanding how managing debt can contribute to your financial foundation.
- Strategies for paying down high interest debts and avoiding unnecessary debt accumulation.

3. Asset Accumulation

Savings vs. Investing
- Distinguishing between saving and investing as methods of accumulating wealth.
- When and how to transition from saving to investing to achieve higher returns.

Diversification
- The principle of diversification in building a strong investment portfolio.
- How to spread risk across different asset classes.

Retirement Accounts
- The significance of retirement accounts like 401(k)s and IRAs.

- Strategies for contributing to retirement accounts to secure your financial future.

4. Financial Education and Resources
Continual Learning
- The importance of staying updated on financial trends and strategies.
- Resources for ongoing financial education, such as books, courses, and websites.

Seeking Professional Advice
- When to consider consulting with financial advisors or experts.
- How to choose a trusted financial professional who aligns with your goals.

Building a strong financial foundation is the initial step on your journey to financial empowerment. By mastering budgeting, effective money management, savings strategies, and asset accumulation, you'll establish the stability and resilience needed to weather financial challenges and seize opportunities. This chapter equips you with the essential knowledge and tools to begin constructing the financial base upon which you'll build your dreams. Your financial success begins with a solid foundation, and you're now well on your way to making it a reality.

- ## **Developing Financial Awareness**

Financial awareness is the cornerstone of making informed financial decisions. It involves understanding your financial situation, knowing where your money comes from and where it goes, and being mindful of your financial goals. In this section, we'll explore the importance of developing financial awareness and practical steps to achieve it.

1. Understanding Your Financial Situation
Income and Expenses
- The significance of knowing your total income, including salary, bonuses, and any additional sources of income.
- How to track and categorize your expenses to gain a clear picture of your spending habits.

Net Worth
- Calculating your net worth by subtracting your liabilities (debts) from your assets (savings, investments, real estate).
- Monitoring your net worth over time to gauge your financial progress.

2. Setting Financial Goals
Short-term and Long-term Goals

- Distinguishing between short term financial goals (e.g., saving for a vacation) and long term financial goals (e.g., retirement planning).
- Prioritizing your goals and creating a timeline for achieving them.

SMART Goals

- The concept of SMART (Specific, Measurable, Achievable, Relevant, Timebound) goals.
- How to structure your financial goals using the SMART criteria.

3. Financial Tracking Tools

Budgeting Apps

- Utilizing budgeting apps and software to monitor your income and expenses.
- Exploring popular budgeting tools and their features.

Spreadsheets and Financial Statements

- Creating personal financial statements using spreadsheets.
- How to interpret and use these statements to gain insights into your financial situation.

4. Regular Financial Check-ins

Monthly Reviews

- The importance of reviewing your financial status regularly, such as on a monthly basis.
- Making adjustments to your budget and financial goals as needed.

Annual Assessments
- Conducting annual assessments of your progress toward long term financial goals.
- Evaluating whether your financial strategies need modification.

5. Savings and Investment Planning

Aligning Savings with Goals
- Ensuring that your savings efforts are directed toward achieving specific financial objectives.
- Adjusting your savings strategy based on your financial awareness.

Investment Tracking
- Monitoring the performance of your investments, including stocks, bonds, and retirement accounts.
- Rebalancing your investment portfolio as your goals and risk tolerance change.

6. Emergency Fund Maintenance

The Role of Emergency Funds

- Understanding the purpose of emergency funds in your overall financial picture.
- Regularly replenishing your emergency fund when necessary.

Developing financial awareness is an ongoing process that empowers you to take control of your financial destiny. By understanding your financial situation, setting clear goals, utilizing tracking tools, and conducting regular check-ins, you'll gain the insight and confidence needed to make informed financial decisions. Financial awareness is the compass that guides you toward your financial aspirations, helping you stay on course and adapt to changing circumstances. As you continue through this journey to financial empowerment, remember that financial awareness is your ally, and it will serve you well as you work toward building wealth and securing your future.

Overcoming Financial Barriers

Financial barriers are challenges that many Black women face in their pursuit of financial success. In this section, we address these barriers head-on and provide strategies to overcome them.

- **Recognizing Systemic Challenges**

Systemic challenges are often deeply ingrained in the economic and societal structures that can disproportionately affect Black women's financial journeys. Recognizing these challenges is the first step in addressing them effectively. In this section, we'll delve into some of the systemic challenges that Black women may face and explore strategies to navigate and overcome them.

1. Racial Wealth Gap
Understanding the Disparity
- Examining the roots of the racial wealth gap and how it has persisted over time.
- Recognizing the impact of this gap on Black women's financial situations.

Strategies for Closing the Gap
- Advocating for policies that aim to reduce wealth disparities.
- Identifying opportunities to build generational wealth and economic stability.

2. Employment Inequities
Wage Disparities

- Acknowledging wage gaps and the impact on income.
- Strategies for negotiating salaries and seeking equitable compensation.

Career Advancement Challenges

- Identifying obstacles to career growth and professional advancement.
- Empowering Black women to overcome these challenges through mentorship, education, and networking.

3. Limited Access to Financial Resources
Barriers to Banking and Loans

- Recognizing the difficulties Black women may face in accessing traditional banking services and loans.
- Exploring alternatives, such as credit unions and community development financial institutions.

Investment Disparities

- Addressing disparities in access to investment opportunities and wealth-building instruments.
- Strategies for diversifying investments and exploring community based initiatives.

4. Historical and Systemic Discrimination
The Legacy of Discrimination

- Understanding how historical discrimination impacts present financial realities.
- Recognizing the importance of acknowledging this legacy.

Advocacy and Empowerment

- Advocating for change through community engagement, policy reform, and awareness campaigns.
- Empowering Black women to challenge systemic discrimination and demand equal opportunities.

5. Educational Barriers

Access to Quality Education

- Recognizing disparities in educational access and quality.
- Strategies for overcoming educational barriers and fostering a love for learning.

Financial Literacy Initiatives

- Supporting financial literacy programs in schools and communities.
- Advocating for education that equips Black women with essential financial knowledge.

6. Community Support and Solidarity

Building Support Networks

- Emphasizing the importance of strong community and support networks.
- Collaborating with like minded individuals and organizations to address systemic challenges collectively.

Recognizing systemic challenges is the first step towards addressing them and forging a path to financial empowerment. By understanding the unique hurdles that Black women may encounter in their financial journeys, you can better navigate these obstacles and work toward solutions. It's important to remember that systemic change often requires collective effort and advocacy. As you continue your journey to financial success, your awareness of systemic challenges can become a driving force for positive change, both on a personal and societal level.

- **Navigating Cultural and Social Pressures**

Cultural and social pressures can significantly influence financial decisions. In this section, we'll explore the impact of these pressures on

Black women's financial journeys and provide strategies for navigating them effectively.

1. Cultural Expectations and Financial Choices

Family Expectations

- Recognizing the role of family expectations in shaping financial decisions.
- Strategies for open communication with family members about financial goals and boundaries.

Cultural Norms

- Identifying cultural norms related to spending, saving, and financial priorities.
- Empowering yourself to make financial choices that align with your personal goals.

2. Consumerism and Lifestyle Pressures

Media Influence

- Understanding how media and advertising can promote consumerism and lifestyle inflation.
- Strategies for resisting the urge to overspend due to external pressures.

Defining Success

- Challenging societal definitions of success that may revolve around material possessions.
- Identifying alternative markers of success that align with your values.

3. Debt and Peer Pressure
Peer Spending Habits
- Recognizing the impact of peer pressure and the desire to keep up with friends' spending.
- Strategies for maintaining financial boundaries while socializing.

Credit Card Debt
- Understanding how easy access to credit can lead to excessive debt.
- Techniques for responsible credit card use and debt management.

4. Educational and Career Choices
Influence of Stereotypes
- Recognizing stereotypes that may influence educational and career choices.
- Strategies for pursuing careers and educational paths that reflect your passions and potential.

Mentorship and Role Models

- The importance of seeking mentorship and guidance from individuals who have overcome similar challenges.
- Finding inspiration and support in successful Black women who have forged their own paths.

5. Community and Support Networks
Building Supportive Communities

- Forming or joining networks that empower and uplift Black women.
- Engaging with organizations and groups that share your financial goals and values.

Mentoring and Mentorship

- Seeking and providing mentorship to foster personal and professional growth.
- Leveraging mentorship relationships for support in navigating cultural and social pressures.

Navigating cultural and social pressures is an integral part of your journey to financial empowerment. By recognizing the external influences that can impact your financial choices and implementing strategies to resist them, you can stay true to your financial goals and values. Remember that your financial decisions should reflect your aspirations and priorities, not the expectations or pressures of others. As you continue on your path to financial success, your ability to navigate cultural and social pressures will empower you to make choices that lead to a more secure and fulfilling future.

- **Overcoming Self-Doubt and Limiting Beliefs**

Self-doubt and limiting beliefs can be significant barriers to financial success. In this section, we'll explore the impact of these internal obstacles and provide strategies for overcoming them to unlock your full financial potential.

1. Identifying Self-Doubt and Limiting Beliefs
Understanding Self-Doubt
- Recognizing the signs and manifestations of self doubt in your financial journey.
- Identifying how self-doubt may have been ingrained over time.

Limiting Beliefs
- Identifying beliefs that restrict your financial aspirations or potential.

- Exploring the origins of these beliefs and their impact on your decisions.

2. Challenging Negative Self-Talk
Cultivating Self-Awareness
- Developing self-awareness to catch negative self-talk in real time.
- Identifying specific phrases or thoughts that contribute to self-doubt.

Positive Affirmations and Mantras
- Using positive affirmations and mantras to counteract negative self-talk.
- Creating a personalized list of affirmations that boost self-confidence.

3. Building SelfConfidence
Setting Achievable Goals
- Establishing financial goals that are both challenging and attainable.
- Celebrating small wins and using them to boost self confidence.

Continuous Learning
- Gaining knowledge and expertise in financial matters.
- Investing in education and skill development to bolster self confidence.

4. Visualizing Success
Mental Imagery

- Practicing visualization techniques that depict your financial success.
- Creating mental images of achieving your financial goals.

Vision Boards
- Constructing vision boards that showcase your financial dreams and aspirations.
- Displaying your vision board in a visible place to serve as a constant reminder.

5. Resilience and Perseverance
Learning from Set-backs
- Viewing financial set-backs as opportunities for growth.
- Analyzing the lessons learned from challenges and applying them to future decisions.

Seeking Support
- Reaching out to a network of supportive friends, family, or mentors.
- Seeking encouragement and guidance during moments of self-doubt.

6. Professional Help and Therapy
Counseling and Therapy

- Exploring the option of counseling or therapy to address deep-seated self-doubt and limiting beliefs.
- Seeking the guidance of mental health professionals to work through psychological barriers.

Overcoming self-doubt and limiting beliefs is an essential part of your journey to financial empowerment. By recognizing and challenging these internal barriers, you can unlock your full potential and make financial decisions that align with your goals and aspirations. Self-confidence, visualization, resilience, and seeking support are key elements in breaking free from self-doubt and limiting beliefs. As you continue on your path to financial success, remember that your mindset and beliefs play a vital role in shaping your financial reality, and with determination and the right strategies, you can conquer these internal obstacles.

In this chapter, we've laid the foundation for your journey towards financial breakthrough. You've discovered the transformative power of financial literacy and explored strategies to overcome the barriers that may have held you back. As you move forward in this book, remember that knowledge is your most potent weapon in the pursuit of financial empowerment. By the end of this chapter, you'll be better equipped to assess your financial landscape, recognize the role of financial literacy, and confront the obstacles that may have stood in your way. Your journey to financial success begins here, and you're well on your way to making your dreams a reality.

Chapter 2

Setting Your Financial Goals

Setting clear and meaningful financial goals is a pivotal step on your journey to financial empowerment. In this section, we'll explore the process of defining and establishing financial objectives that will drive your success.

Setting your financial goals is a foundational step in your journey to financial empowerment. By defining your dreams and aspirations, creating SMART goals, prioritizing them, and breaking them down into manageable steps, you'll create a roadmap for achieving financial success. Remember that your financial goals should reflect your unique vision and values. As you continue on your path, stay committed to these goals, track your progress, and remain adaptable in the face of changing circumstances. Your financial goals are the compass that will guide you towards the life you envision, where dreams become a vivid and triumphant reality.

Defining Your Dreams and Aspirations

Before you embark on your financial journey, it's crucial to have a clear understanding of your dreams and aspirations. These aspirations will serve as the driving force behind your financial goals. In this section, we'll explore the process of defining your dreams and aspirations:

1. Self-Reflection

- Take Time for Introspection: Begin by setting aside dedicated time for self-reflection. Find a quiet, comfortable space where you can think deeply about your life and what truly matters to you.

- Explore Your Passions: Consider your passions and interests. What activities or pursuits make you feel most alive and fulfilled? What brings you joy and satisfaction?

- Personal Values: Reflect on your core values and principles. What do you hold dear, and how do these values influence your life choices?

2. LongTerm Vision

- Envision Your Ideal Life: Create a mental picture of your ideal life. Where do you see yourself in 5, 10, or 20 years? What does this life look like in terms of your career, family, lifestyle, and overall well being?

- Retirement and Legacy: Think about your retirement and what you'd like to achieve during this phase of your life. Consider the legacy you want to leave for future generations.

3. Clarify Financial Aspirations
- Financial Independence: What does financial independence mean to you? It might entail the ability to cover all your expenses without financial stress.

- Debt Freedom: Do you aspire to be debt free? This could include paying off loans, mortgages, or credit card debt.

- Specific Financial Milestones: Are there specific financial milestones you want to achieve, such as buying a home, starting a business, or funding your children's education?

4. Lifestyle Choices
- Travel and Experiences: Consider the places you want to visit and the experiences you'd like to have. Travel,

adventure, and cultural experiences may be a part of your dreams.

- Health and Wellness: Think about your health and wellbeing. How does maintaining good physical and mental health factor into your aspirations?

5. Relationships and Community

- Family and Relationships: Consider your family and relationships. What role do these connections play in your life, and how do they influence your dreams?

- Community and Giving Back: Think about your community involvement and philanthropic aspirations. How do you want to contribute to your community or society as a whole?

6. Recording Your Aspirations

- Journaling: Consider keeping a journal where you can document your dreams, aspirations, and long term vision.

- Vision Board: Create a vision board with images, quotes, and symbols that represent your aspirations. Display it in a visible place to serve as a constant reminder.

Defining your dreams and aspirations is a deeply personal and introspective process. It forms the foundation for your financial goals and decisions. By gaining clarity on what truly matters to you, you'll be better equipped to set meaningful financial objectives that align with your vision of a fulfilling life. Your dreams are the compass that guides your financial journey, helping you stay focused, motivated, and true to your values. As you continue on this path to financial empowerment, remember that your aspirations are the driving force behind your efforts to build wealth and create the life you desire.

Creating SMART Financial Goals

SMART goals are **Specific**, **Measurable**, **Achievable**, **Relevant**, and **Timebound**. They provide a clear and structured framework for setting objectives that are more likely to be achieved. In the context of financial empowerment, here's how to create SMART financial goals:

1. Specific Goals

- Define Your Financial Objectives: Clearly specify what you want to achieve. For example, "I want to save money" is vague, but "I want to save $10,000 for a down payment on a house" is specific.

- Identify the Purpose: Explain why this goal is important to you. Understanding the purpose behind your goal can provide motivation and focus.

- Avoid Ambiguity: Make sure your goal is unambiguous, leaving no room for misinterpretation.

2. Measurable Progress

- Quantify Your Goal: Define how you will measure your progress. In the example of saving for a down payment, the amount to be saved, $10,000, is a measurable quantity.

- Set Milestones: Break your goal into smaller, measurable milestones. For instance, you can aim to save $2,500 every three months.

- Use Numbers and Dates: Be clear about the specific numbers and dates involved. This makes it easier to track your progress.

3. Achievable Goals

- Assess Feasibility: Ensure that your financial goal is attainable within your current circumstances. It's okay to aim high, but your goal should still be realistic.

- Consider Resources: Determine what resources, such as time, money, or skills, you need to achieve your goal. Are these resources available or attainable?

- Plan Your Path: Outline the steps and actions you need to take to reach your goal. Create a roadmap for achievement.

4. Relevant to Your Life

- Align with Your Values: Confirm that your goal is relevant to your life and values. Your financial goals should reflect your personal aspirations and priorities.

- Avoid Pursuing Unrelated Goals: Ensure your financial goals directly contribute to your long term vision and purpose.

5. **Time-Bound Objectives**
- Set a Deadline: Define a clear timeframe for achieving your goal. For instance, "I will save $10,000 for a down payment on a house within three years."

- Periodic Check-ins: Establish a schedule for regular check ins and assessments of your progress. Are you on track to meet your deadline?

- Adjust as Needed: Be prepared to adapt your goal if circumstances change. A time bound goal allows you to evaluate and adjust as necessary.

Example: A SMART Financial Goal

"I will save $10,000 for a down payment on a house within the next three years. To achieve this, I will save $2,500 every three months and regularly track my progress. This goal is important to me because homeownership aligns with my long term vision of financial stability and security."

By creating SMART financial goals, you can increase the likelihood of success. These goals provide a clear path, allow you to measure your progress, and keep you focused on what truly matters to you in your financial journey.

Chapter 3

Building a Strong Financial Foundation

A strong financial foundation is the cornerstone of financial stability and success. It provides you with the stability and resilience to navigate life's challenges and seize opportunities.

By focusing on these fundamental aspects, you'll be well on your way to building a strong financial foundation that supports your financial wellbeing and long term success. A solid financial foundation provides the stability and security needed to achieve your financial goals and make your dreams a reality. In this section, we'll explore the essential components of building a strong financial foundation:

Budgeting and Money Management

Effective budgeting and money management are fundamental skills for achieving financial success and building a strong financial foundation. In this section, we'll delve into the key principles and strategies for budgeting and managing your finances:

1. Creating a Budget

- **Income Assessment**

Begin by determining your total income, including your salary, bonuses, investments, and any other sources of earnings.

- **Expense Categorization**

Categorize your expenses into essentials (e.g., housing, groceries, utilities) and nonessentials (e.g., entertainment, dining out). This helps you understand your spending patterns.

- **Setting Financial Goals**

Define your financial goals, both shortterm and longterm. Your budget should align with these goals.

2. Expense Tracking

- **Monitor Your Spending**

Keep a close eye on your daytoday spending. Use a mobile app, spreadsheet, or dedicated budgeting software to track expenses.

- **Identify Areas to Cut Costs**

Review your spending habits to identify areas where you can cut costs. This might include reducing unnecessary subscriptions or finding more affordable alternatives.

3. Emergency Funds

- **Importance of Emergency Funds**

Recognize the significance of having an emergency fund. This fund acts as a financial safety net for unexpected expenses, such as medical bills or car repairs.

- **Creating an Emergency Fund**

Set a goal to save a certain amount, like three to six months' worth of living expenses, in your emergency fund. Start by saving a small portion of your income each month.

4. Debt Management

- **Understanding Debt Types**

Differentiate between various types of debt, such as high interest credit card debt and lower interest student loans. Prioritize paying off high interest debt.

- **Debt Repayment Plan**

Create a debt repayment plan that specifies how much extra money you can allocate to paying off your debt each month.

5. Savings Strategies for Success

- **Setting Savings Goals**

Define your savings goals, such as saving for a vacation, a new car, or retirement. These goals provide motivation to save.

- **Automated Savings**

Automate your savings by setting up regular transfers from your checking account to your savings account or investment portfolio. This ensures consistent saving.

6. Continuous Review and Adjustment

- **Monthly Reviews**

Regularly review your budget to track your progress and make adjustments as needed. Ensure you're sticking to your spending plan.

- **Annual Assessments**

Conduct annual assessments to evaluate your financial progress and adjust your budget and goals accordingly.

Effective budgeting and money management provide you with financial control, help you achieve your goals, and ensure that you're making the most of your income. By implementing these strategies, you'll be on the path to financial stability and success.

Saving Strategies for Success

Savings are the building blocks of financial security and achieving your long term goals. In this section, we'll explore effective strategies for saving money and growing your financial resources:

1. Setting Savings Goals

- Specific Objectives

Define clear and specific savings goals. Whether it's building an emergency fund, buying a house, or funding your children's education, having specific goals provides direction.

- Short-term and Long-term Goals

Differentiate between short term goals (e.g., a vacation in a year) and longterm goals (e.g., retirement in several decades). Prioritize your goals based on timelines.

2. Automated Savings

- **Pay Yourself First**

Make savings a priority by setting up automated transfers from your checking account to your savings or investment accounts as soon as you receive your paycheck. This "pay yourself first" approach ensures that you save consistently.

- **Take Advantage of Employer Benefits**

If your employer offers retirement savings plans, such as a 401(k), take full advantage of them. Contribute at least enough to receive any employer match, as this is essentially free money.

3. Debt Management

- **High interest Debt First**

Prioritize paying off high interest debt, such as credit card balances, before aggressively saving. The interest on debt can often exceed investment returns.

- **Balance Debt Repayment and Savings**

While paying off debt is essential, consider balancing it with some level of savings to ensure you're building a financial cushion.

4. Financial Mindset

- **Frugal Living**

Embrace a frugal lifestyle by finding ways to reduce unnecessary expenses. This extra money can be redirected toward savings.

- **Budgeting and Tracking**

Continuously track your expenses and adhere to your budget. This practice helps you identify areas where you can cut costs.

5. Diversification of Savings

- **Emergency Fund**

Establish an emergency fund with three to six months' worth of living expenses. This fund serves as a financial safety net for unexpected events.

- **Retirement Accounts**

Contribute regularly to retirement accounts like a 401(k) or IRA. These accounts offer tax advantages and help you build long term wealth.

- **Investments**

As your savings grow, consider diversifying into investments like stocks, bonds, or real estate to potentially earn higher returns.

6. Regular Review and Adjustment

- Monthly Savings Review

Periodically review your savings goals and assess your progress. Make adjustments to your savings plan as needed.

- Annual Assessments

Conduct annual assessments to evaluate your overall financial situation and make changes to your savings and investment strategy.

Consistent saving is a key element of financial success. By setting clear goals, automating your savings, effectively managing debt, adopting a frugal mindset, and diversifying your savings, you'll be well on your way to achieving financial security and building the wealth needed to accomplish your dreams.

Chapter 4

Investing for Wealth

Investing is a powerful tool for building wealth and achieving your long term financial goals. In this section, we'll explore the key principles and strategies for successful investing:

1. Understanding Investment Basics

- Asset Classes

Learn about different asset classes, such as stocks, bonds, real estate, and alternative investments. Understand the risk and return profiles of each.

- Risk Tolerance

Assess your risk tolerance to determine how much risk you're comfortable taking with your investments. Your risk tolerance influences your asset allocation.

- Time Horizon

Consider your investment time horizon. Longer time horizons generally allow for a more aggressive investment approach.

2. Diversification

- **Spread Risk**

Diversify your investment portfolio by holding a mix of different asset classes. Diversification can help spread risk and reduce the impact of market fluctuations.

- **Asset Allocation**

Create a well balanced asset allocation strategy based on your financial goals, risk tolerance, and time horizon.

3. Investment Accounts

- **Tax-Advantaged Accounts**

Take advantage of tax-advantaged investment accounts, such as 401(k)s, IRAs, and 529 plans. These accounts offer tax benefits that can boost your returns.

- **Taxable Investment Accounts**

Consider opening taxable investment accounts for additional flexibility and to invest beyond the limits of tax advantaged accounts.

4. Regular Contributions

- **Consistent Investments**

Make regular contributions to your investment accounts, whether it's monthly, quarterly, or annually. Consistent investments can lead to long term wealth accumulation.

- **Dollar-Cost Averaging**

Implement dollar cost averaging, which involves investing a fixed amount at regular intervals, regardless of market conditions. This strategy can reduce the impact of market volatility.

5. LongTerm Perspective

- **Patience**

Understand that investing is a long term endeavor. Be patient and avoid making impulsive decisions based on short term market fluctuations.

- **Compounding**

Leverage the power of compounding. Over time, your returns can generate additional earnings, accelerating your wealth growth.

6. Continuous Learning

- **Educate Yourself**

Continually educate yourself about investment options, strategies, and market trends. Staying informed is crucial for making informed investment decisions.

- **Seek Professional Advice**

When necessary, consider consulting with a financial advisor or investment expert for guidance on complex investment matters.

7. Risk Management

- **Emergency Fund**

Ensure you have an adequate emergency fund in place before making substantial investments. This safeguards you against unexpected financial setbacks.

- **Asset Protection**

Consider strategies for protecting your assets, such as insurance and estate planning.

Successful investing requires discipline, knowledge, and a long term perspective. By understanding investment basics, diversifying your portfolio, taking advantage of tax advantaged accounts, making regular contributions, and staying patient, you can create a path to building wealth over time. Investing is a key component of your financial journey, helping you achieve your long term financial goals and secure your future.

Investing Basics and Strategies

Investing is a crucial component of building wealth and achieving long term financial goals. Let's delve into the fundamental investing principles and strategies:

<u>Investing Basics</u>

1. Risk and Return

- Understand the relationship between risk and return. Generally, higher returns are associated with higher risks.

- Consider your risk tolerance when making investment decisions.

2. Asset Classes

Know the major asset classes:

- Stocks

Represent ownership in a company and can offer potential high returns but come with higher volatility.

- Bonds

Are debt securities and typically provide more stable, fixed returns.

- Real Estate

Includes physical properties and real estate investment trusts (REITs).

- Cash and Cash Equivalents

Like savings accounts or money market funds, which offer stability but lower returns.

3. Diversification

- Diversify your investments across different asset classes to reduce risk.

- A well-diversified portfolio can help cushion the impact of market fluctuations.

4. Time Horizon

- Consider your investment time horizon, which affects your risk tolerance and investment strategy.

- Longer time horizons can allow for more aggressive investments.

Investment Strategies

1. Buy and Hold

This strategy involves buying investments with the intent of holding them for an extended period, typically years or even decades. It works well for longterm investors and capitalizes on the power of compounding.

2. Dollar-Cost Averaging

Invest a fixed amount of money at regular intervals (e.g., monthly). This approach reduces the impact of market volatility and can lead to more favorable average prices over time.

3. Value Investing

Seek undervalued assets, such as stocks or real estate, with the potential for long term growth. Value investors look for opportunities that the market may have overlooked.

4. Growth Investing

Focus on assets that have the potential for significant growth. Growth investors often prioritize companies with promising products, services, or innovations.

5. Income Investing

Aim to generate regular income from investments, typically through dividend paying stocks, bonds, or real estate. This strategy is favored by those seeking a consistent cash flow.

6. Passive vs. Active Investing

- **Passive Investing**

Involves investing in index funds or exchange traded funds (ETFs) that track market benchmarks. It's a hands off approach that often comes with lower fees.

- **Active Investing**

Requires making more frequent investment decisions, trying to outperform the market.

Active investors often trade individual stocks or engage in more complex strategies.

7. LongTerm Perspective

Maintain a long term perspective and avoid reacting to short term market fluctuations. Emotional reactions to market volatility can lead to suboptimal investment decisions.

8. Regular Monitoring and Rebalancing

Periodically review and adjust your portfolio to ensure it aligns with your investment goals and risk tolerance. Re-balancing may involve buying or selling assets to maintain your desired allocation.

Remember that there is no one size fits all investment strategy. Your choice should align with your financial goals, risk tolerance, and time horizon. It's advisable to diversify your investments and seek professional advice when necessary, especially for complex investment decisions. Successful investing is a continuous learning process, and staying informed is key to making informed choices.

Building a Diverse Investment Portfolio

A diverse investment portfolio is essential for managing risk and pursuing long term financial success. Here's how to build a well diversified portfolio:

1. Asset Allocation

- Stocks

Allocate a portion of your portfolio to stocks. These can offer higher returns but come with higher risk. The allocation depends on your risk tolerance and investment goals.

- Bonds

Include bonds in your portfolio for stability and income. The proportion of bonds can vary based on your risk profile and investment horizon.

- Real Estate

Consider real estate investments, such as real estate investment trusts (REITs), which can provide diversification and potential income.

- Cash and Equivalents

Maintain some liquidity by keeping a portion of your portfolio in cash or cash equivalents like money market funds.

2. Diversify Within Asset Classes

- ● Stock Diversification

When investing in stocks, diversify across different sectors (e.g., technology, healthcare, consumer goods) and geographic regions. Avoid putting all your funds into a single stock.

- ● Bond Diversification

Diversify your bond holdings by investing in bonds with various maturities and credit qualities. This spreads risk.

- ● Real Estate Diversification

Consider different types of real estate investments, such as residential, commercial, or industrial properties.

3. International Exposure

Invest globally to reduce dependence on a single economy. Consider international stocks, bonds, and even global mutual funds or exchange-traded funds (ETFs).

4. Asset Allocation Strategy

Create an asset allocation strategy that aligns with your risk tolerance and investment goals.

Rebalance your portfolio periodically to maintain the desired allocation.

5. Risk Tolerance and Goals

Your risk tolerance and goals should guide your asset allocation. For example, if you have a higher risk tolerance and long term goals, you may allocate more to stocks.

6. Regular Review and Adjustment

Periodically review your portfolio to ensure it remains diversified according to your strategy. Adjust the allocation as needed based on your changing financial situation.

7. Consider Professional Guidance

If you're unsure about how to diversify or select specific investments, consider seeking advice from a financial advisor. They can help tailor your portfolio to your unique circumstances.

8. Stay Informed

Continually educate yourself about investment options and market trends. Staying informed is crucial for making informed decisions about your portfolio.

A diverse investment portfolio can help mitigate risk while providing opportunities for growth and income. By balancing your investments across asset classes, diversifying within those classes, and considering your risk tolerance and financial goals, you can build a portfolio that aligns with your long term financial objectives.

Chapter 5

Income Generation and Entrepreneurship

Generating additional income streams and exploring entrepreneurship can significantly boost your financial well-being. Here are strategies and insights for income generation and entrepreneurship:

Income Generation

1. Side Hustles and Gig Economy

Explore side hustles or participate in the gig economy. These opportunities can provide extra income and often offer flexibility.

2. Freelancing

Leverage your skills by freelancing in your field of expertise. Websites and platforms like Upwork, Fiverr, or Freelancer can connect you with potential clients.

3. Investment Income
Generate income from investments, such as dividends from stocks, interest from bonds, or rental income from real estate properties.

64

4. Passive Income

Create sources of passive income, such as writing a book, developing an online course, or building a blog or YouTube channel that generates advertising or affiliate income.

Entrepreneurship

1. Identify a Niche

Find a niche or market gap where your skills, passion, and expertise align. Identifying an underserved audience can be the foundation of a successful business.

2. Business Plan

Develop a comprehensive business plan that outlines your business idea, target market, competition, revenue model, and financial projections.

3. Financial Planning

Prepare for the financial aspects of entrepreneurship. Ensure you have a financial cushion to cover startup costs and support yourself during the early stages of your business.

4. Legal Structure

Choose the appropriate legal structure for your business, such as sole proprietorship, LLC, or corporation. Consult with legal and tax professionals for guidance.

5. Market Research

Conduct thorough market research to understand customer needs, preferences, and potential competition. This data is crucial for making informed decisions.

6. Branding and Marketing

Build a strong brand and marketing strategy. Create a unique value proposition and consider online and offline marketing channels.

7. Financial Management

Implement sound financial management practices. Keep a close eye on expenses, budget effectively, and track income and cash flow.

8. Adaptability

Be adaptable and ready to pivot if necessary. Market conditions and customer preferences can change, so your business should be flexible.

9. Customer Service

Provide exceptional customer service. Happy customers are more likely to become repeat clients and refer others to your business.

10. Continuous Learning

Stay updated on industry trends, best practices, and emerging technologies. Continuous learning is vital for staying competitive.

11. Network and Seek Support

Build a network of contacts in your industry and seek advice from mentors or business associations. They can offer valuable insights and support.

Remember that entrepreneurship comes with both opportunities and risks. It's essential to be well prepared, have a clear vision, and be willing to put in hard work and dedication. Income generation and entrepreneurship can open up new avenues for financial growth and independence.

Exploring Multiple Streams of Income

Diversifying your income with multiple streams can provide financial stability and help you achieve your goals. Here are various ways to explore multiple streams of income:

1. Side Hustles and Gig Work

Consider part-time jobs or freelance work in areas where you have skills and expertise.

2. Investments

Generate income from investments, such as dividends from stocks, interest from bonds, or rental income from real estate properties.

3. Passive Income

Develop passive income sources, like creating and selling digital products, investing in a blog or YouTube channel, or participating in affiliate marketing.

4. Rental Income

If you have extra space in your home, consider renting it out through platforms like Airbnb or long term rentals.

5. Online Courses and Consulting

Offer online courses or consulting services related to your field of expertise.

6. Create and Sell

Consider creating and selling physical or digital products, such as art, crafts, ebooks, or printables.

7. Participate in the Sharing Economy

Rent out your car, equipment, or other assets on plat-forms like Turo or Airbnb.

8. Passive Investments

Invest in real estate crowd-funding plat-forms, peer to peer lending, or robo advisors for automated investing.

9. Dividend Stocks

Invest in dividend-paying stocks to receive regular income in the form of dividends.

10. Affiliate Marketing

Promote products or services on your blog, website, or social media and earn commissions on sales or leads.

11. Dropshipping or Ecommerce

Start an online store and sell products without holding inventory through drop-shipping.

12. Licensing Your Work

License your creative work, such as photographs, music, or art, for use in various media or by other creators.

13. Real Estate Investment Trusts (REITs)

Invest in REITs, which allow you to earn rental income from a diversified portfolio of properties without direct ownership.

14. Write and Publish a Book

Write and self publish a book, which can provide ongoing royalties.

15. Divide Your Skills

Utilize your skills in multiple ways, such as offering coaching, speaking engagements, or workshops.

16. Online Marketplaces

Sell products on online marketplaces like Amazon, eBay, or Etsy.

17. Teaching and Tutoring

Offer tutoring services or teach classes online or in your local community.

18. Participate in Clinical Trials or Surveys:

Participate in clinical trials, surveys, or focus groups that offer compensation.

19. Write for Publications

Write articles or contribute to magazines, websites, or newspapers.

20. Franchise Ownership

Consider owning a franchise in an industry that interests you.

Remember that building multiple streams of income takes time and effort. Start by exploring opportunities aligned with your skills, interests, and resources. Diversifying your income can provide financial security, reduce risk, and bring you closer to your financial goals.

Starting and Scaling Your Business

Starting and growing a business can be a rewarding endeavor, but it requires careful planning and execution. Here are the key steps to start and scale your business:

Starting Your Business

1. Business Idea and Research
Begin with a solid business idea. Research the market to understand your target audience, competition, and industry trends.

2. Business Plan

Create a comprehensive business plan that outlines your business goals, strategies, financial projections, and marketing plan.

3. Legal Structure

Choose a legal structure for your business, such as a sole proprietorship, LLC, partnership, or corporation. Consult with legal and tax professionals to make the right choice.

4. Financing

Determine how you'll finance your business. Options include personal savings, loans, investors, or crowdfunding.

5. Business Name and Registration
Register your business name and acquire any necessary permits or licenses.
6. Business Location

Decide on a physical location if needed, or consider starting as an online or home based business.

7. Build a Team

If your business requires it, hire and build a team with the skills and expertise necessary for your success.

8. Business Website and Online Presence

Create a professional website and establish a strong online presence through social media and online marketing.

9. Product or Service Development

Develop your product or service, ensuring it meets the needs of your target market.

10. Marketing and Sales Strategy

Develop a marketing and sales strategy to attract and retain customers. Consider various marketing channels, such as social media, content marketing, email marketing, and advertising.

11. Financial Management

Implement sound financial management practices. Keep track of expenses, income, and cash flow.

Scaling Your Business

1. Customer Base Expansion

Focus on growing your customer base by reaching new markets and expanding your customer reach.

2. Diversification

Explore new product or service offerings to cater to a broader audience or meet changing market demands.

3. Increase Productivity

Implement strategies and tools to increase productivity and efficiency within your business operations.

4. Hiring and Training

Continue to hire and train the right talent to support business growth.

5. Financial Resources

Secure additional financing or investment to support scaling efforts.

6. Technology and Automation

Embrace technology and automation to streamline processes and reduce manual tasks.

7. Market Expansion

Explore new markets or geographic areas for expansion.

8. Customer Loyalty

Focus on building customer loyalty and offering excellent customer service to retain existing clients.

9. Strategic Partnerships

Collaborate with other businesses or form strategic partnerships that can help your business grow.

10. Monitor and Adapt

Continuously monitor key performance indicators (KPIs) and adapt your business strategies based on data and insights.

Scaling a business requires a clear growth plan and a willingness to adapt to changing circumstances. Ensure you maintain a strong focus on financial management, customer service, and strategic decision making as you work towards expanding your business. Remember that growth can be a gradual process, and it's essential to manage it effectively to maintain long term success.

Chapter 6

Navigating Debt and Credit

Managing debt and credit responsibly is crucial for your financial well-being. Navigating debt and credit responsibly requires discipline and vigilance. By creating a plan to manage and reduce debt, maintaining good credit habits, and seeking professional guidance when necessary, you can take control of your financial situation and work toward a more secure financial future.

Managing Debt Effectively

Effectively managing debt is essential for maintaining your financial wellbeing and achieving your long term goals. Here are steps to help you manage debt effectively:

1. Assess Your Debt

Start by creating a comprehensive list of all your debts, including credit card balances, loans, and mortgages. Note the outstanding balances, interest rates, and monthly payments for each.

2. Prioritize High-Interest Debt

Focus on paying down high-interest debt first. This type of debt, such as credit card balances, can be the most costly.

3. Create a Repayment Plan

Develop a debt repayment plan that includes how much you'll pay each month toward each debt. Consider using the debt snowball or debt avalanche method to determine the order in which you pay off your debts.

4. Budgeting and Expense Tracking

Create a detailed budget to track your income and expenses. This will help you allocate a portion of your income to debt repayment.

5. Emergency Fund

While paying down debt, aim to build and maintain an emergency fund to cover unexpected expenses. This will prevent you from resorting to additional debt in times of need.

6. Additional Income

Look for ways to increase your income, such as taking on a part time job, freelancing, or selling items you no longer need. Use the extra income to accelerate your debt payments.

7. Debt Consolidation and Refinancing

Explore options for consolidating or refinancing your debt to lower interest rates and simplify your payments. Be cautious about taking on new debt while doing so.

8. Avoid Accumulating More Debt

Make a commitment to avoid taking on new debt, especially for nonessential purchases, while you're paying down existing debt.

9. Financial Counseling

Consider seeking the guidance of a financial counselor or advisor to help create a tailored debt management plan.

10. Stay Committed

Reducing debt takes time and discipline. Stay committed to your repayment plan and avoid the urge to accumulate more debt.

11. Monitor Your Progress

Regularly track your progress in paying down your debts. Celebrate each milestone, no matter how small, to stay motivated.

Managing debt effectively is a gradual process that requires patience and diligence. By creating a clear repayment plan, budgeting wisely, and seeking additional income, you can reduce your debt and work toward a more financially secure future.

Building and Maintaining Good Credit

Good credit is essential for obtaining favorable loan terms, securing rental agreements, and more. Here are steps to build and maintain good credit:

Building Good Credit

1. Open a Credit Account

To build credit, you need to have credit accounts in your name. Start with a secured credit card or a credit builder loan if you don't have a credit history.

2. Pay Bills on Time

Pay all your bills, including credit card payments, loans, and utilities, on time. Consistently making payments is one of the most critical factors in building good credit.

3. Use Credit Responsibly

Use your credit accounts responsibly. Avoid carrying high balances, and keep your credit utilization (credit used versus available credit) low, ideally below 30%.

4. Diversify Credit Types

Have a mix of different types of credit accounts, such as credit cards, installment loans, and retail accounts.

5. Credit Monitoring

Regularly monitor your credit report to check for inaccuracies or identity theft. You can access one free credit report per year from each of the major credit bureaus.

Maintaining Good Credit

1. Pay Bills on Time, Every Time

Continue to make all payments on time. Late payments can have a negative impact on your credit score.

2. Manage Credit Card Balances

Keep your credit card balances in check and avoid carrying high levels of debt. Reducing credit card balances can positively affect your credit utilization.

3. Don't Close Old Accounts

Keep old credit accounts open, even if you no longer use them. The length of your credit history contributes to your credit score.

4. Limit New Credit Applications

Avoid applying for multiple credit cards or loans in a short period, as this can negatively affect your credit score.

5. Regularly Use Your Credit

Use your credit accounts periodically to show responsible credit use. Inactivity on an account can lead to it being closed by the creditor.

6. Communicate with Creditors

If you're facing financial difficulties, contact your creditors to discuss temporary arrangements or hardship programs. This proactive approach can help prevent negative marks on your credit report.

7. Credit Monitoring

Continue to monitor your credit report for accuracy and any signs of identity theft or fraud.

Remember that building and maintaining good credit is a long-term endeavor. Responsible credit management, payments, and wise credit utilization are key to ensuring your credit remains strong. A good credit score can provide opportunities and save you money in the future.

Chapter 7

Protecting Your Financial Future

Securing your financial future involves various aspects of financial planning and protection. Here are steps to help safeguard your financial wellbeing:

1. Emergency Fund

Build and maintain an emergency fund with at least three to six months' worth of living expenses. This financial safety net can cover unexpected setbacks like medical bills or job loss.

2. Insurance Coverage

Evaluate your insurance needs, including health, life, disability, auto, home, and, if applicable, business insurance. Ensure you have adequate coverage to protect against unexpected events.

3. Retirement Planning

Contribute regularly to retirement accounts, such as a 401(k) or IRA. Establish a clear retirement plan and set goals for your retirement savings.

4. Estate Planning

Create a comprehensive estate plan that includes a will, power of attorney, and healthcare directives. Consult with an attorney to ensure your assets are distributed according to your wishes.

5. Debt Management

Manage and reduce high interest debt. Develop a debt repayment plan and avoid taking on new debt whenever possible.

6. Diversification

Diversify your investment portfolio to reduce risk. Consider spreading investments across various asset classes, such as stocks, bonds, and real estate.

7. Continuous Learning

Stay informed about financial matters and make informed decisions about your investments, insurance, and financial planning.

8. Avoid Impulsive Decisions

Avoid impulsive financial decisions, especially in times of market volatility. Make decisions based on your long term goals and financial plan.

9. Regular Assessments

Periodically review your financial plan and make adjustments as your circumstances change. This includes updating your budget and investment strategy.

10. Professional Guidance

Seek advice from financial advisors, attorneys, or accountants when making significant financial decisions or managing complex financial matters.

11. Protect Against Identity Theft

Be vigilant about safeguarding your personal and financial information. Use strong, unique passwords, monitor your accounts for unauthorized activity, and be cautious with sharing personal information online.

12. Keep Important Documents Secure

Keep financial documents, such as tax records, bank statements, and investment statements, in a secure place. Consider digitizing important documents and using secure cloud storage.

13. Prepare for the Unexpected

Develop contingency plans for unforeseen circumstances, such as a natural disaster or sudden loss of income.

14. Set Financial Goals

Clearly define your financial goals, both shortterm and longterm. Having goals can help you stay motivated and on track.

Safe-guarding your financial future requires a combination of careful planning, financial discipline, and protection against unforeseen events. By taking these steps, you can help secure your financial wellbeing and work toward achieving your financial goals.

Insurance and Risk Management

Insurance is a critical component of financial planning, helping protect you and your assets from unforeseen risks. Here's how to effectively manage insurance and risk:

Types of Insurance

1. Health Insurance

Ensure you have health insurance coverage that meets your needs. It provides financial protection against medical expenses and can safeguard your long term financial well being.

2. Life Insurance

Life insurance can provide financial security for your loved ones in the event of your passing. Consider your family's financial needs when choosing the type and amount of coverage.

3. Auto Insurance

Auto insurance is mandatory in most places. Make sure you have appropriate coverage to protect against accidents and liability.

4. Homeowners or Renters Insurance

If you own a home, homeowners insurance safeguards your property and possessions. Renters insurance offers protection for tenants. Review your coverage regularly to ensure it's up to date.

5. Disability Insurance

Disability insurance provides income replacement if you're unable to work due to a disability. It's essential for protecting your earning potential.

6. Umbrella Insurance

An umbrella policy provides additional liability coverage beyond your standard policies, such as auto and homeowners insurance. It's useful for high networth individuals.

Risk Management

1. Risk Assessment

Assess potential risks in your life and financial situation. This includes considering health, property, income, and other areas of vulnerability.

2. Emergency Fund

Build and maintain an emergency fund to cover unexpected expenses that insurance may not fully protect against.

3. Regular Review

Periodically review your insurance policies to ensure they align with your current needs and financial situation. Update coverage as needed.

4. Coverage Limits

Consider the coverage limits and deductibles of your policies. Higher coverage limits may provide better protection but can increase premiums.

5. Comparative Shopping

Shop around for insurance to find the best coverage at the most competitive rates. Don't settle for the first quote you receive.

6. Seek Professional Advice

Consult with insurance professionals, such as independent agents or brokers, for expert guidance on selecting the right policies.

7. Educate Yourself

Understand the terms, conditions, and exclusions in your insurance policies. Being well informed can help you make the most of your coverage.

8. Claim Management

If you need to make a claim, follow the appropriate process and document all relevant information. Promptly report claims to your insurance provider.

Insurance and risk management are fundamental aspects of financial planning. By having the right insurance coverage and a well thought out risk management strategy, you can protect your assets, health, and financial future from unexpected events.

Estate Planning and Wealth Preservation

Estate planning is vital for ensuring your assets are distributed according to your wishes and preserving your wealth for future generations. Here are essential steps in estate planning and wealth preservation:

1. Create a Will

Draft a will that clearly outlines how you want your assets to be distributed after your passing. Appoint an executor to carry out your wishes.

2. Consider a Trust

Depending on your financial situation and goals, consider creating a trust. Trusts offer more control over how assets are managed and distributed and can help avoid probate.

3. Designate Beneficiaries

Ensure all your financial accounts, insurance policies, and retirement accounts have designated beneficiaries. This ensures a smooth transfer of assets without going through the probate process.

4. Medical and Financial Power of Attorney

Designate someone you trust to make medical and financial decisions on your behalf in case you become incapacitated.

5. Guardianship for Minor Children

If you have minor children, designate a guardian in your will who will be responsible for their care in the event of your passing.

6. Plan for Taxes

Be aware of estate and inheritance taxes. Consult with a tax professional to develop strategies to minimize tax liabilities.

7. Regularly Review and Update Your Plan

Life circumstances change, so your estate plan should be reviewed and updated regularly. Make adjustments for major life events, such as marriage, divorce, births, or deaths in the family.

8. Charitable Giving

If you have charitable intentions, include them in your estate plan. You can leave assets to your chosen charities or establish a charitable foundation.

9. Consider Life Insurance

Life insurance can provide a source of funds for your beneficiaries and help cover any estate taxes.

10. Seek Professional Guidance

Consult with an estate planning attorney to ensure your plan aligns with your objectives and is legally sound.

11. Preserve Wealth Through Financial Management

Implement sound financial management practices to preserve your wealth over time. Diversify your investments, minimize unnecessary expenses, and consider inflation when planning for the future.

12. Long-term Care Planning

Consider how you'll address long term care needs as you age, including the potential use of long term care insurance.

Estate planning and wealth preservation are essential to protect your assets and ensure they benefit your heirs or chosen causes as you intend. It's a complex process that often requires professional assistance to navigate successfully. By planning and taking steps to safeguard your wealth, you can create a legacy that aligns with your values and goals.

Chapter 8

Retirement Planning and Early Retirement

Early retirement can be an appealing goal, but it requires careful planning to ensure financial security. It is achievable with careful planning, disciplined saving, and strategic investment. While it offers more time for leisure and personal pursuits, it requires thorough financial preparation to ensure a comfortable and secure retirement.

Crafting Your Retirement Vision

Creating a clear and inspiring retirement vision is the first step in planning for a fulfilling retirement. Here's how to craft your retirement vision:

1. Reflect on Your Goals

Think about what you want to achieve in retirement. Consider both financial and nonfinancial goals, such as traveling, pursuing hobbies, spending time with family, or contributing to causes you care about.

2. Visualize Your Ideal Retirement

Imagine your ideal retirement lifestyle. Where would you like to live? What activities do you want to engage in? How do you envision spending your time?

3. Financial Assessment

Determine the financial resources needed to support your retirement vision. This includes estimating retirement expenses and assessing your retirement savings and investments.

4. Set Specific Goals

Break down your retirement vision into specific, achievable goals. For example, you may set a goal to retire at a certain age, have a specific retirement income, or travel to a particular destination.

5. Plan for Health and Wellness

Consider your physical and mental health in retirement. Plan for activities that promote wellbeing, such as exercise, healthy eating, and staying socially engaged.

6. Create a Bucket List

Develop a retirement bucket list of experiences and goals you want to accomplish. This can add excitement and purpose to your retirement years.

7. Social and Family Considerations

Think about how your retirement plans will impact your relationships and family. Discuss your retirement vision with your loved ones and consider their goals and needs as well.

8. Volunteer and Giving Back

Explore opportunities for volunteer work or giving back to your community. Many retirees find fulfillment in contributing to causes they are passionate about.

9. Lifelong Learning

Consider how you'll continue learning and growing in retirement. Pursue educational interests or engage in new hobbies and activities.

10. Review and Adjust

Periodically review and adjust your retirement vision as your circumstances and priorities change. Flexibility is key to adapting to life's evolving landscape.

11. Seek Professional Guidance

Consult with a financial advisor to align your retirement vision with your financial plan. They can help you create a roadmap to achieve your goals.

Crafting your retirement vision is a personal and creative process. It's about defining the life you want to lead in retirement and working towards it. With a clear vision and a well thought-out plan, you can look forward to a retirement that aligns with your aspirations and dreams.

Strategies for Retiring on Your Terms
Retiring on your terms requires careful planning and financial preparation. Here are key strategies to help you achieve the retirement you desire:

1. Define Your Retirement Goals

Clearly outline your retirement goals, including when you want to retire, your desired lifestyle, and financial objectives.

2. Create a Retirement Budget

Develop a detailed budget for retirement that accounts for your expected expenses, including housing, healthcare, leisure activities, and travel. Be realistic in your estimates.

3. Assess Your Retirement Savings

Review your retirement savings and investments. Ensure you have a diversified portfolio that balances risk and potential returns.

4. Maximize Retirement Accounts

Contribute to retirement accounts like 401(k)s and IRAs to take advantage of tax benefits and grow your savings.

5. Pay Off HighInterest Debt

Reduce high interest debt, such as credit card balances, before retiring to decrease financial burdens.

6. Healthcare Planning

Understand healthcare costs during retirement, including Medicare and supplemental insurance. Budget for medical expenses and potential long term care needs.

7. Consider Your Social Security Strategy

Decide when to start claiming Social Security benefits, considering factors like your financial needs and life expectancy.

8. Diversify Income Sources

Explore diverse income sources, such as investment income, part time work, or rental properties, to supplement your retirement income.

9. Evaluate Housing Options

Assess your housing needs and whether downsizing or relocating could reduce living expenses.

10. Professional Guidance

Consult with a financial advisor to create a retirement plan tailored to your goals and circumstances.

11. Emergency Fund

Maintain an emergency fund to cover unexpected expenses during retirement, reducing the need to dip into your savings.

12. Lifestyle Adjustments

Be open to lifestyle adjustments that allow you to retire comfortably. This may involve living more modestly or delaying retirement by a few years.

13. Regular Financial Assessment

Continuously monitor your financial situation and make adjustments as needed. Periodic reviews help ensure your plan aligns with your goals.

14. Early Retirement Considerations

If you're considering early retirement, assess the financial independence needed to retire comfortably. Build a plan that accommodates your long-term financial needs.

15. Legal and Estate Planning

Address estate planning by creating a will, establishing powers of attorney, and designating beneficiaries. Consult with an attorney to ensure your assets are distributed according to your wishes.

Retiring on your terms requires a combination of clear financial planning, prudent saving and investing, and a deep understanding of your retirement goals. By taking these steps, you can work toward achieving the retirement lifestyle you desire.

Chapter 9

Overcoming Financial Challenges

Financial challenges are a common part of life, but with strategic planning and determination, you can overcome them. Here are steps to help you address and conquer financial difficulties:

1. Assess Your Situation

Begin by taking a close look at your financial situation. Identify the specific challenges you're facing, whether it's debt, low income, high expenses, or something else.

2. Create a Budget

Develop a comprehensive budget that tracks your income and expenses. This will provide a clear understanding of where your money is going and help you identify areas for improvement.

3. Prioritize Essential Expenses

Prioritize essential expenses like housing, utilities, groceries, and healthcare. Ensure these are covered before allocating funds to discretionary spending.

4. Reduce Discretionary Spending

Cut back on non essential expenses, such as dining out, entertainment, and shopping. Redirect these funds toward addressing your financial challenges.

5. Debt Management

If debt is a major challenge, create a debt repayment plan. Focus on paying off high interest debts first and consider debt consolidation or refinancing options.

6. Emergency Fund

Establish and maintain an emergency fund to cover unexpected expenses. Having this financial safety net can prevent further financial setbacks.

7. Increase Income

Explore opportunities to increase your income, such as taking on a part time job, freelancing, or selling items you no longer need.

8. Seek Professional Advice

Consult with a financial advisor or counselor for guidance in addressing your specific financial challenges. They can provide tailored solutions.

9. Negotiate Bills

Negotiate with service providers, like your internet or cable company, to secure better rates. You can often lower your bills by simply asking.

10. Education and Skills

Consider further education or skill development to enhance your earning potential. Learning new skills can open up better job opportunities.

11. Avoid Impulsive Spending

Practice discipline in your spending habits and avoid impulsive purchases that can exacerbate financial challenges.

12. Consistent Review

Continually review your financial situation, adjust your budget as needed, and celebrate small victories along the way.

13. Emotional Well-being

Pay attention to your emotional and mental wellbeing. Financial challenges can be stressful, so seek support or counseling if necessary.

14. Long-term Planning

Think about long-term financial planning, including retirement and estate planning, even as you work to overcome immediate challenges.

15. Stay Positive and Patient

Overcoming financial challenges may take time. Maintain a positive outlook and stay patient as you work toward your financial goals.

Financial challenges can be daunting, but with determination and strategic steps, you can make progress toward financial stability. The key is to take a proactive approach, create a plan, and persistently work towards your goals.

Breaking Through Limiting Beliefs

Limiting beliefs can hinder your personal and financial growth. Here's how to break through these mental barriers:

1. SelfAwareness

Start by identifying your limiting beliefs. Reflect on the thoughts and beliefs that have held you back from pursuing your financial goals.

2. Challenge Negative Beliefs

Question the validity of your limiting beliefs. Are they based on facts or assumptions? Challenge them with evidence to the contrary.

3. Positive Affirmations

Replace negative self-talk with positive affirmations. Repeat empowering statements to reinforce a positive mindset.

4. Visualize Success

Visualize yourself achieving your financial goals. This mental imagery can boost your confidence and motivation.

5. Surround Yourself with Positivity

Seek out positive influences and avoid people or situations that reinforce your limiting beliefs. Surround yourself with those who support your growth.

6. Education and Learning

Invest in your knowledge and skills. Education can boost your confidence and help you overcome self doubt.

7. Goal Setting

Set clear, achievable financial goals. Working towards these goals can replace doubts with a sense of purpose.

8. Break Down Goals

Divide your goals into smaller, manageable tasks. Achieving these smaller milestones can build your confidence over time.

9. Embrace Failure as Learning

Don't fear failure; see it as an opportunity to learn and grow. Mistakes are part of the journey toward success.

10. Seek Support

Talk to a mentor, coach, or therapist who can provide guidance and support in addressing limiting beliefs.

11. Take Action

Action is one of the most powerful ways to break through limiting beliefs. Start taking small steps towards your financial goals, even if it feels uncomfortable at first.

12. Celebrate Achievements

Acknowledge and celebrate your successes, no matter how small. This positive reinforcement can help build your confidence.

13. Practice Self compassion

Be kind to yourself. Avoid self criticism and self judgment. Embrace self compassion as you work on your growth.

14. Persistence

Breaking through limiting beliefs may not happen overnight. Stay persistent and committed to your personal and financial development.

15. Keep a Growth Mindset

Adopt a growth mindset, where you believe that your abilities and intelligence can be developed with effort and learning.

Remember that changing limiting beliefs is an ongoing process. By taking consistent, positive actions and challenging negative thoughts, you can build a mindset that empowers you to pursue your financial goals and achieve the success you desire.

Handling Financial Setbacks with Resilience
Financial setbacks are a part of life, but with resilience and a strategic approach, you can navigate them successfully. Here are steps to help you handle financial setbacks with resilience:

1. Acknowledge Your Feelings

It's natural to feel a range of emotions when facing a financial setback. Allow yourself to acknowledge and process these feelings.

2. SelfCompassion

Be kind to yourself and avoid self blame. Understand that financial setbacks happen to many people and do not define your worth.

3. Assess the Situation

Take a close look at the nature and extent of the financial setback. Understand the causes and implications of the setback.

4. Create a Financial Snapshot

Develop a comprehensive picture of your current financial situation, including income, expenses, assets, and debts.

5. Prioritize Expenses

Prioritize essential expenses like housing, utilities, groceries, and healthcare. This ensures that your basic needs are met during the setback.

6. Develop a Budget

Create a detailed budget to manage your finances during the setback. Make necessary adjustments to cut discretionary spending.

7. Emergency Fund

Utilize your emergency fund to cover immediate expenses if you have one. If not, consider building one for future financial protection.

8. Seek Support

Lean on your support network. Share your situation with trusted friends or family members who can offer emotional and possibly financial support.

9. Contact Creditors

If you have debts, contact your creditors to discuss temporary arrangements or hardship programs. Many creditors are willing to work with you during difficult times.

10. Consider Financial Assistance

Explore government assistance programs or community resources that may be available to help with specific financial setbacks.

11. Maintain Clear Communication

Keep open lines of communication with family members or dependents who may be affected by the financial setback. Discuss adjustments as a team.

12. Review and Adjust Your Goals

Temporarily adjust your financial goals to reflect your current situation. Be flexible in your expectations.

13. Seek Professional Guidance

Consult with a financial advisor or counselor for personalized advice on how to recover from the setback.

14. Future Planning

Use the setback as an opportunity to reevaluate your long term financial plans, including emergency savings, insurance, and investments.

15. Build Resilience

Cultivate a resilient mindset that embraces challenges as opportunities for growth and learning.

Financial setbacks can be challenging, but they also provide opportunities for personal and financial growth. By facing setbacks with resilience, you can emerge stronger and better prepared to handle future financial challenges.

Chapter 10

Building a Supportive Financial Network

A strong financial network can provide you with valuable resources, support, and guidance. Here's how to build and nurture a supportive financial network:

1. Identify Your Needs

Determine your financial goals, challenges, and the specific types of support you require. This will guide you in finding the right people to connect with.

2. Family and Friends

Start by involving your close friends and family. Share your financial goals and challenges with them. They can offer emotional support and share their experiences.

3. Join Financial Communities

Participate in financial forums, groups, or social media communities focused on personal finance. These spaces can be excellent sources of advice and support.

4. Attend Financial Workshops and Seminars

Seek out local or online financial workshops and seminars. These events can connect you with like-minded individuals and experts.

5. Professional Advisors

Consider hiring professionals like financial advisors, accountants, or lawyers for expert guidance.

6. Networking Events

Attend networking events related to your field of interest or financial goals. You can meet potential mentors, partners, or investors.

7. Online Platforms

Explore online platforms and apps dedicated to personal finance and investment. Some platforms allow you to connect with financial experts and peers.

8. Social Media
Follow financial influencers, bloggers, and experts on social media platforms. Engage in

discussions and ask questions when you need advice.

9. Support Groups

Look for support groups or organizations that focus on specific financial challenges, such as debt management or investment.

10. Mentorship

Seek out a financial mentor who has experience in areas you're interested in. A mentor can provide personalized guidance and motivation.

11. Be Open and Vulnerable

Don't be afraid to share your financial goals and challenges with others. Transparency can lead to meaningful connections.

12. Be a Good Listener

Actively listen and learn from others. Your network can provide valuable insights and experiences.

13. Reciprocate Support

Be willing to support others in your network when they need help. Building a supportive community is a two way street.

14. Regular Communication

Maintain regular communication with the members of your network. Keep them updated on your progress and challenges.

15. Respect Diverse Perspectives

Your network may have diverse opinions and perspectives. Respect these differences and be open to alternative viewpoints.

A supportive financial network can play a significant role in helping you achieve your financial goals, providing guidance, encouragement, and accountability. Building and nurturing such a network takes time and effort, but it can be a valuable resource on your financial journey.

Leveraging Mentors and Networks

Mentors and professional networks can greatly accelerate your personal and financial growth. Here's how to effectively leverage them:

1. Identify Your Goals

Clearly define your financial and career goals. Knowing what you want to achieve will help you find the right mentors and networks.

2. Seek Potential Mentors

Look for individuals who have achieved the goals you aspire to reach. These individuals can serve as mentors and provide guidance and advice.

3. Network Strategically

Attend industry specific events, conferences, and seminars to connect with professionals in your field. Join online forums and groups related to your interests.

4. Join Professional Associations

Many industries have professional associations or organizations. Becoming a member can provide access to valuable networks and resources.

5. Ask for Introductions

Don't be afraid to ask for introductions from your current contacts. Your friends and colleagues may know someone who can be a valuable mentor.

6. Be Proactive

Take the initiative to reach out to potential mentors or network contacts. Send personalized messages or emails expressing your interest in connecting.

7. Mutual Benefit

Approach mentorship and networking as a two way street. Offer something in return, even if it's just a willingness to learn and grow.

8. Listen and Learn

When connecting with mentors or network contacts, be a good listener. Learn from their experiences and ask thoughtful questions.

9. Respect Their Time

Be respectful of your mentors' time. Schedule meetings or interactions at their convenience, and be punctual.

10. Set Clear Goals

Share your goals and expectations with your mentors. Discuss what you hope to achieve through the mentorship relationship.

11. Stay Committed

Show dedication to your mentorship or network relationships. Consistency is key to building trust and long lasting connections.

12. Attend Mentorship Programs

Some organizations offer formal mentorship programs. These can be a structured way to connect with experienced professionals.

13. Stay Active Online

Participate in online discussions, comment on relevant articles, and share your expertise.

This can help you get noticed and connect with like minded professionals.

14. Join Mastermind Groups

Consider joining or forming a mastermind group of individuals with similar goals. This provides a supportive and collaborative environment.

15. Pay It Forward

Once you've gained experience and expertise, consider becoming a mentor or supporting others in your network.

Mentors and professional networks can provide guidance, opportunities, and a sense of community. Leveraging these relationships effectively can be a significant asset in your personal and financial growth journey.

The Power of Community and Collaboration
Community and collaboration can be powerful forces in achieving your personal and financial goals. Here's how you can harness this power:

1. Supportive Communities

Join or create communities of like minded individuals who share your interests and goals. Whether it's a local group or an online forum, these communities can provide motivation and encouragement.

2. Knowledge Sharing

Collaborate with others to exchange knowledge and expertise. You can learn from their experiences and insights, and in turn, offer your own valuable knowledge.

3. Accountability Partners

Find accountability partners who can help you stay on track with your goals. Sharing your progress and setbacks with someone else can boost your commitment.

4. Resource Pooling

Collaborate to pool resources and share costs. This can be particularly helpful for investment opportunities or starting a business.

5. Collective Learning

Engage in group learning experiences, such as workshops or courses. Learning together can be more motivating and provide diverse perspectives.

6. Networking

Attend networking events and connect with professionals in your industry. Building a strong professional network can open doors to opportunities and collaborations.

7. Crowd-sourcing

Utilize crowd-sourcing platforms to gather ideas, funds, or solutions from a large community. Crowd-funding, for example, can help finance projects.

8. Idea Generation

Collaborate on brainstorming and idea generation. Fresh perspectives from a group can lead to innovative solutions and opportunities.

9. Volunteering

Give back to your community by volunteering your skills and time. Not only is it a fulfilling experience, but it can also lead to connections and opportunities.

10. Emotional Support

Lean on your community for emotional support during challenging times. Having people who understand your journey can provide comfort and resilience.

11. Partnerships

Seek out potential partners for your business ventures. Collaboration with complementary businesses can lead to mutual growth.

12. Mentorship and Coaching

Join mentorship or coaching programs to receive guidance from experienced professionals. Their expertise can be invaluable.

13. Strategic Alliances

Form strategic alliances with other businesses or organizations that share common goals. This can lead to joint ventures and expanded reach.

14. Share Successes and Failures

Share your experiences, both successes and failures, with your community. It can inspire others and foster a culture of learning.

15. LongTerm Relationships

Nurture and maintain your community and collaborative relationships for the long term. Building lasting connections can lead to ongoing opportunities.

The power of community and collaboration lies in the collective strength, knowledge, and resources of a group of individuals working together toward common goals. By actively participating in such networks, you can amplify your efforts and increase your chances of achieving personal and financial success.

Conclusion

In conclusion, the journey to financial success is a dynamic and multifaceted one, shaped by a combination of knowledge, mindset, and practical strategies. This book, "Black Girl's Manual to Financial Breakthrough: Guide to Build Wealth, Retire in Advance, and Make Your Dream Life a Reality," has explored various aspects of financial empowerment and wealth-building for women of color.

We've delved into understanding the importance of financial literacy and the impact of financial knowledge on decision making. We've recognized the barriers and systemic challenges that can stand in the way of financial progress, while also addressing cultural and social pressures that may affect financial choices.

Overcoming self-doubt and limiting beliefs is a critical step on this journey, as is setting clear financial goals and defining dreams and aspirations. We've emphasized the importance of creating SMART financial goals and building a strong financial foundation, complete with budgeting, saving, investing, and debt management strategies.

We've discussed the value of multiple income streams, entrepreneurship, and navigating the world of business. The importance of managing debt effectively and building and maintaining good credit has been highlighted, as well as protecting your financial future through insurance and risk management.

Estate planning and wealth preservation are crucial for ensuring that your assets benefit you and your loved ones as you intend. Retirement planning, including the possibility of early retirement, has been explored, along with the importance of crafting a retirement vision and practical strategies for retiring on your terms.

We've addressed the challenges of handling financial setbacks with resilience and breaking through limiting beliefs. Finally, we've discussed the power of community and collaboration in achieving personal and financial goals.

The key take-away is that financial empowerment is within reach for every woman, and the knowledge, tools, and strategies outlined in this book can serve as a guide to making your financial dreams a reality. Remember that your financial journey is unique, and it's essential to adapt these principles to your specific circumstances.

With a growth mindset, determination, and the support of mentors and networks, you have the potential to break through barriers, build wealth, retire comfortably, and create the life you desire. Financial empowerment is a journey, and this book is your companion along the way. May it inspire and empower you to achieve your financial breakthrough.

About the Author

The author of "Black Girl's Manual to Financial Breakthrough: Guide to Build Wealth, Retire in Advance, and Make Your Dream Life a Reality" is Bianca Robert. Bianca Robert is a recognized expert in personal finance, wealth building, and financial empowerment. She has dedicated her career to helping women of color overcome financial barriers, achieve their financial goals, and lead lives of abundance and security.

Bianca Robert has a deep passion for financial education and empowerment. Her journey in the field of personal finance began with a commitment to addressing the unique challenges faced by women of color when it comes to building wealth and achieving financial freedom. She has since become a prominent voice in the financial empowerment community, using her expertise to inspire and guide others on their financial journeys.

In addition to her writing, Bianca Robert has conducted workshops, seminars, and speaking engagements, sharing her knowledge and insights on personal finance with diverse audiences. Her practical, relatable approach to financial empowerment has resonated with many, making her a trusted resource and mentor in the field.

Bianca Robert is also actively involved in philanthropic efforts, working to provide financial education and support to underserved communities. Her dedication to making a positive impact on the financial well-being of women of color has earned her recognition and respect within the financial and empowerment communities.

"Black Girl's Manual to Financial Breakthrough" is a culmination of Bianca Robert's expertise and passion for financial empowerment. It serves as a comprehensive guide to help women of color overcome financial challenges, build wealth, retire comfortably, and turn their dreams into reality. Through her work, Bianca Robert aims to empower women to take control of their financial destinies and achieve the life they envision.